Florien Giauque

A Manual for Road Supervisors in Ohio

Florien Giauque

A Manual for Road Supervisors in Ohio

ISBN/EAN: 9783337420123

Printed in Europe, USA, Canada, Australia, Japan

Cover: Foto ©Lupo / pixelio.de

More available books at **www.hansebooks.com**

A MANUAL

FOR

ROAD SUPERVISOR

IN OHIO

CONTAINING THE PROVISIONS OF LAW RELATING TO THE D
OF THESE OFFICERS

WITH,

NOTES OF DECISIONS, NUMEROUS FORMS,
AND PRACTICAL SUGGESTIONS.

FOURTH REVISED EDITION.

BY

FLORIEN GIAUQUE,

THE " REVISED STATU OHIO," AUTHO
MENT OF DECEDENTS' "A MAN
SIGNEES," "A M GUARDIAN
TRU

PREFACE

AND EXPLANATORY MATTER.

In this little manual, the author has tried to furnish supervisors a practical and cheap guide—to tell them, in plain language, what their duties are under the codified laws, and how to perform these duties. To this end, he has tried to give the substance of these laws, and of all reported decisions of our courts bearing on the subject, to give complete references to these laws and decisions, to furnish all necessary forms, to make such practical suggestions as seemed useful, to give a good index to all of this, and to arrange, classify, and have it published in such a way that it will be easy to refer to, and to carry about the person, or suitable to have in the office or library.

The numbers at the beginning of each paragraph indicate the number of that paragraph in the chapter, each chapter having its own series of such numbers. The numbers in large figures inclosed in parentheses, found either at the end or in the body of the paragraph, refer to the sections of the law as numbered in the Revised Statutes of the State of Ohio. Paragraphs or parts of paragraphs not followed by such numbers are generally the suggestions of the writer. The small figures refer to the notes below, which generally consist of decisions of our own Supreme Court, and have, therefore, all the force of law. The decisions quoted from the Ohio Reports are indicated thus: 19 Ohio, 867, and would mean that the case referred to is found in the nineteenth volume of the Ohio Reports, on page 867; and 26 Ohio St. 196, would mean that this case is found in the twenty-sixth volume of the Ohio State Reports, page 196. W. means Wright's Report.

CINCINNATI, *June*, 1882

F. G.

(iii)

PREFACE TO FOURTH EDITION.

Since issuing the third edition of this book, the legislature has repealed all laws requiring persons to labor two days each year on the public roads (see note on page 12), thereby radically changing the entire system of road repairs, at least in theory. But said roads must still be kept in repair and free from obstructions, under the direction of the road supervisor, by means of road taxes, which may be paid in money, or worked out as formerly. These changes in his duties, and the new duties imposed on him in late years as to stock running at large on the roads, as to hedges on the wayside; as to weeds, briers, brush, etc., in the roadway; as to drift in streams, ditches, etc.; as to the making and cleaning of ditches themselves; new road construction under his direction, etc., make him one of the most important of our lesser officers. It is therefore highly necessary that he have at hand the means of knowing what these duties now all are, and how to go about fulfilling them, and also what are such no longer. To this end this new edition is prepared.

As explained in the Preface to the first edition, numbers in the body or at the end of a paragraph, and in parentheses, for instance (4889), show in what section of the statute the law in that paragraph can be found. If such numbers are now followed by others, for instance (4889, 91 O. L. 355), it means that the law is from section 4889, as amended in volume 91 Ohio Laws, page 355.

Laws which refer to one county or neighborhood only are not given, and have not been, in any edition.

FLORIEN GIAUQUE.

CINCINNATI, *July,* 1894.

(iv)

ROAD SUPERVISORS.

CHAPTER I.

RELATING TO ELECTION, OATH, BOND, ETC., OF SUPERVISOR.

1. *Township trustees must divide township into road districts, etc.* On the first Monday of March of each year, the township trustees must, 1st, divide their township into road districts, when not already so divided, or alter the existing districts, as they may deem proper; 2d, have a description of such districts, as so made or altered, entered in the proper township record; 3d, give notice of the number of supervisors to be chosen in the township. They must also cause due notice of the time and place for the election of supervisors to be given. (1457, 1503, 1445, 1446.)

2. *Supervisors are township officers when elected, etc.* Supervisors of roads are regular township officers,[1] and must be elected at the annual township election, on the first Monday of April, in the same way as other township officers are chosen (1442. 89 O. L. 195; 1448, 90 O. L. 144); subject, however, to the following special provisions:

3. *Who may be supervisor, and how elected.* Every supervisor of roads must be a resident of the district for which he is elected; and no elector shall vote for more than one supervisor of roads, or for any person for that office who is not an actual resident of the district in which said elector resides; and if a ballot contains more than one named for the office of supervisor, or if it appears to the satisfaction of the judges of election that an elector has voted for any person for that office other than for the district in which such elector resides, such vote, as to that office, must be deemed void; and if, on counting the votes, it appears that there were more votes given for supervisor

---

(1) A supervisor of roads is an officer, within the meaning of section 20 (now sec. 6908), which provides as follows: "That if any person shall abuse any judge or justice of the peace, abuse or resist any sheriff, constable, or other officer in the execution of his office, the person so offending," etc. Woodworth v. State, 26 Ohio S. 196. (See paragraph 17, Chapter IV.)

To constitute the offense of re-isting an officer, under the above section, it is not necessary that the officer should be assaulted, beaten, or abused. Ib.

(1)

of a district than there were resident electors of such district voting at such election, the judges must declare the election, as to that district, void; and the vacancy must be filled by the trustees as in other cases of vacancy. (1456.)

4. *Penalty for refusing to serve, how collected.* A person elected or appointed supervisor, who neglects or refuses to serve, must forfeit and pay to and for the use of his township the sum of two dollars, to be recovered by an action before a justice of the peace of said township;[1] and the township clerk must, in the name of said township, collect said money, by suit, if necessary, and pay it over, when collected, to the township treasurer; but no person shall be compelled to serve in a township office two years in succession. (1449.)

5. *Vacancies, and how filled.* In case no annual election is held, because enough voters do not assemble to hold it, or if, by reason of non-acceptance, death, or removal of a person chosen supervisor at an election duly held, or when, from any other cause, a vacancy occurs in the office of supervisor, the trustees of the township must appoint some suitable person to fill the vacancy, who must, before entering upon the duties of his office, take an oath to faithfully and impartially discharge the duties of his office, and shall be under the same restrictions and penalties as though he had been duly elected and qualified. (4741, 1451, as am. 87 v. 119.)

7. *Oath and bond.* Each person chosen or appointed to an office under the constitution or laws of this state, must take an oath of office.[2] (2) The township clerk must, within ten days after the election or appointment of the supervisor, notify him thereof, by the constable, in the manner required by law, and require him to appear before such clerk or other officer authorized by law to administer oaths, and take the required oath of office, and give bond, within ten days after such election or appointment. (1453.)

8. It is best to take this oath before the clerk, as it must be recorded by him, no matter who administers it. If administered by some other officer, the law imposes upon such officer the duty of making a certificate of the oath to such clerk, who must then record the oath. (2, 5, 1453, 1454.) But this is more troublesome, is liable to be more expensive, and to be in part neglected, if not done before the clerk himself.

9. A supervisor's oath is in substance as follows: (3)

---

(1) A person refusing to serve as supervisor, after being elected or appointed, is liable to a fine of two dollars. But he can not be compelled to accept any other township office at the same time he holds the office of supervisor. Hartford v. Bennett, 10 Ohio S'. 441.
(2) The Constitution of Ohio (art. XV. sec. 7) also requires such oath.

The State of Ohio,   }
—— County, —— Township. } ss.

Before me, C—— D——, clerk of said township, personally came A—— B——, who, being duly sworn according to law, says that he will support the constitution of
the United States and the constitution of the State of
Ohio; and that he will faithfully discharge his duties as
supervisor of road district No. ——, of —— township, ——
county, Ohio, during his continuance in said office, and
until his successor is chosen and qualified.

                              A——, B——.

Sworn to before me, and signed in my presence, on this
—— day of ——, A. D. 18—.

                C—— D——, Township Clerk.

10. The failure of the supervisor to take the oath does
not affect the liability of his sureties. (2)

11. Before entering upon the discharge of his duties,
each supervisor of roads must give bond, with sureties
approved by the trustees, in such sum as they determine, payable to them, and conditioned for the faithful
performance of his duties, which bond must be deposited
with the clerk; and if he fails to take the oath and
give the bond required, within ten days after his election
or appointment, he must be deemed to have declined to
accept, and the vacancy must be filled as in other cases.
(1515; 19, 1453, 1455.)

12. *Form of bond.* The following is the form of a supervisor's bond:

Know all men by these presents: That we, A—— B——,
as principal, and C—— D—— and E—— F—— as sureties,
are held and firmly bound under the trustees of ——
township, in the county of ——, and State of Ohio, in the
sum of one hundred dollars, to be paid to the said trustees
of the township aforesaid, for the payment whereof well
and truly to be made, we jointly and severally bind our-
selves, our heirs, executors, and administrators firmly by
these presents.

This done and signed by us, this —— day of ——, A. D.
18—.

The condition of the above obligation is such, that
whereas the said A—— B—— has been duly elected and
qualified as supervisor of road district No. ——, of ——
township, —— county, and State of Ohio, for the term of
one year from the —— day of April, A. D. 18—, and until
his successor is elected, or appointed, and qualified.

Now, if the said A—— B—— shall faithfully perform

his duties as said officer, then this obligation will be void;
otherwise to be and remain in full force and effect.

A—— B——,   [SEAL.]
C—— D——,   [SEAL.]
E—— F——,   [SEAL.]

The sureties on the above bond approved by us:

G—— H——,
I—— K——, } Trustees of said Township.
L—— M——,

13. The township trustees should hold a meeting within
the time required by law for approving the bonds, for
the express purpose of approving bonds and other similar
business, and of this meeting the supervisor elect should
be officially notified by the clerk. The supervisor should
go to this meeting with his sureties, and there request the
clerk to make out his bond. The clerk is, perhaps, not
bound to do this, but it is customary, and generally well
for him to do so. For this purpose he should be supplied by
the trustees with printed blank bonds, which need but little
time and labor to fill up accurately, and so as to be good
and valid at law. The bond having been duly executed,
may then be filed; and the oath of office having been administered to the new supervisor, he can then receive such
instructions, laws, etc., as the clerk may have to give him.
14. *Serves how long.* The person elected or appointed,
as above described, and having duly filed a proper bond and
taken the required oath, is fully installed into the office
of supervisor of roads for his district, to serve till the next
regular spring election, and until his successor, then
elected or soon after appointed, is qualified. (8, 11, 1448,
90 O. L. 144; 1450, 1451.)
15. *In hamlets.* The trustees of hamlets may appoint an
elector of their corporation as marshal, who may be by ordinance required to act as supervisor; but, whenever they
provide by ordinance for the separation of the offices of
marshal and supervisor, they must annually, while such
ordinance is in force, select an elector as supervisor; and
they may, in either case, prescribe his duties and compensation, and may remove him and appoint another, at their
discretion. (1700, as am. 77 v. 15.) The marshal, when
he acts as supervisor, must act under the direction of the
trustees, and be paid out of the proper hamlet treasury, or
treasuries, the same compensation allowed to other supervisors; and where the offices of marshal and supervisor
are separated, the supervisor must perform his duties, be
paid in the same manner, and receive the same compensation, as the marshal when acting as supervisor. (1703, as
am. 86 v. 252.)

CHAPTER II.

SUPERVISORS' WORK, DUTIES AND POWERS GENERALLY.

1. *Duty of supervisor as to opening roads.* The law provides that every supervisor must open, or cause to be opened, all public roads and highways which are laid out and established in his road district.[1] (4715.) But new state and county roads are now opened by the county commissioners by contract. See par. 8 of this chapter.

2. But if a state road, or any part of one, has been laid out for ten years, or a county road, or any part of one, has been authorized, and has remained unopened for public use for seven years after being ordered or authorized to be so opened, the law declares such road to be vacated by lapse of time and non-user.[2] (4636, 4668, 89 v. 126.)

3. *Public roads classified and defined.*—For the purpose of assisting the supervisor to know what his duties are, the "public roads and highways," that are in some way considered such by the laws of Ohio, may be divided into:[3]

First. *Toll roads,* owned by incorporated companies, and for traveling over which pay is collected at toll-gates, or by other means. With these the supervisor has nothing whatever to do.[4]

---

(1) A supervisor is a local ministerial officer, whose authority and duties to open, repair, and control public roads extends only to the roads within his own district. Grove *v.* Mikesell, 13 Ohio St. 158.

A supervisor is, in this state, regarded as a ministerial officer, whose duties and authority are limited and prescribed by statute, and which, for the most part, are confined to his own particular district. His duties generally are to open and keep in repair and unobstructed the public roads in his particular district not owned or operated under private charters or by incorporated companies. His powers and authority have always, in this state, been particularly prescribed by statute. And under these statutes, we understand that the courts of this state have always recognized the right of supervisors to a very liberal exercise of an honest discretion in the discharge of their official duties. It would be most unreasonable, under such statutory provisions, to hold a supervisor to a rigid exactitude in the use of the most appropriate means for the discharge of his duties. Grove *v.* Mikesell, 13 Ohio St. 158.

See also notes on page 9.

(2) The statute providing that county roads shall be vacated by non-user for seven years applies only to roads that have been authorized, but never opened. Peck et al. *v.* Clark et al., 19 Ohio, 367.

The limitation prescribed in that section of law applies to roads authorized but never opened, and not to roads which have been opened and partially obstructed by a landholder fencing in a portion of the same. McClelland *v.* Miller, 28 Ohio St. 488.

The public right to a highway may be lost by non-user. The law would raise a presumption of an extinguishment of the right, when the road has been abandoned for a long period, but where there has been a continued use of a highway, and the width has been encroached upon by the adjacent owner for eighteen years, the right is not lost, and the supervisor may open such road to its full width. Fox *v.* Hart, 11 Ohio, 414.

(3) An exhaustive classification would include more than these. But for the purposes of this volume, this is not required.

(4) A supervisor of highways has no jurisdiction or power over turnpikes or plank roads constructed by incorporated companies, and placed by law under their control; nor could he justify interference with such roads, although it should be directed by the township trustees. He is

Second. *Streets and alleys in cities and incorporated villages.* But these streets and alleys are under the exclusive control of the councils of the municipal corporations in which they are situate, and over them the supervisor has no control whatever,[1] except as stated in paragraph 18, Chapter III.

Third. *Improved roads.* These are classed by the Revised Statutes as turnpikes (free), one-mile assessment pikes, two-mile assessment pikes, and unfinished and abandoned turnpikes, and are defined by statute in the following provision : " All macadamized or graveled roads which are free roads, whether constructed under general or local laws by taxation or assessment, or both, or converted by purchase or otherwise from a-toll road into a free road under any law, and all turnpike roads, or parts thereof, unfinished or abandoned by any turnpike company, and appropriated or accepted by the commissioners of the county, shall be kept in repair as provided in this chapter." (4876.) The supervisor's duty relating to these improved roads is treated of in Chapter III of this work.

Fourth. *Ordinary free roads,* classed by law and generally known as state roads, county roads, and township roads.

4. *Township roads.* The law expressly declares township roads " to be public highways " (4686, 89 O. L. 304). It also defines them by providing, in substance, that if any person wishes to have a township road laid out from any person's farm or dwelling place, or from any mill or house of public worship, or to any cemetery or burial ground, or to a public road, or from one public road to intersect another, or from any tract of wild land or timber land, or from any stone quarries, coal mines, or mineral lands (other than gas or oil lands) to a railroad or railroad station, or from a railroad station, to a township, county, or state road, or sawmill, he may petition the township trustees for it, etc. (4672, 88 O. L. 561). It then provides how such a road may be established, and that when so established, it "shall be considered a private or township road, subject to be kept open and in repair at the expense of the applicants for the same, or otherwise, as provided by law." (4677, as am., 79 O. L. 72.)

5. *Supervisor must keep certain township roads in repair.* But it further provides, that a township road which commences in a state, turnpike, township, or county road, or at a railroad station, and is not less than thirty feet in width, and passes on and intersects another state, turnpike, county, or township road, must be opened and kept in repair by the

bound to know what roads belong to the public and what to such trustees. Chagrin Falls & Cleveland Plankroad Co. *v.* Cane et al., 2 O. St. 419.

(1) § 2640. When any part of a road district is annexed to a city, that part of the road lying in the annexed territory passes out of the jurisdiction of the supervisor, and into the control of the corporation. Steubenville *v.* King, 23 Ohio St. 610.

supervisor in whose district it may be situated, in whole or
in part. (4678, as am., 77 O. L. 72.)

6. In certain cases, state, county, and township roads
may be improved under the instructions of the supervisor.
See pars. 57 to 61, this chapter.

7. *State and county roads.* From the foregoing it is seen
that the supervisor has to do chiefly with the state and
county roads. In fact, the great majority of supervisors in
the state have no jurisdiction over, and no work to do on
any others; and on these, only, as a general rule, after
they have been not only "laid out and established," but
also opened. His duties will *generally* be confined to keeping them in proper repair and free from obstruction.

8. *As to establishing, opening, straightening, vacating, etc.,
roads, supervisor's course.* The law provides how state,
county, and other roads may be " laid out and established,"
and also how they may be turned, widened, or narrowed,
vacated, etc., and what proceedings must be had in such
cases. These proceedings are numerous and long, and
involve and require petitions, bonds, viewers, etc. But
these are the affairs of those desiring the road or the
changes mentioned, and with them the supervisor has
nothing to do. After all these proceedings are had, and
the county commissioners make the proper entries on their
minutes, establishing or changing the road as above mentioned, and after the time required by law has passed, they
must now[1] have such roads opened by contract. (See §
4650, as am., 90 O. L. 119; § 4634.)

9. In the case of township roads, the law provides that
(after the petition, bond, etc., and other preliminary steps
are attended to) if the township trustees deem the establishing of such a road reasonable and just, they must order
the clerk of the township to record the report of the
viewers, and issue their order to the petitioners, or to the
proper supervisor where it is made his duty to open the road,
to open it to the width named in the report of the viewers.
(4677, as am., 88 O. L. 349.) The proceedings are substantially the same in case of widening, narrowing, changing,
or vacating township roads, so far at least as the supervisor
is concerned. (See 4681–4685.) The trustees, through the
township clerk, should then order, in writing, the supervisors of the proper road districts to open or change such
road as directed, particularly and definitely describing the
line of the road to be opened or the change to be made;
and till then, the supervisor should do nothing at all
toward opening or changing such roads.

(1) Formerly, §4650 provided that after the establishment of the road,
it should thenceforth " be considered a public highway, *and the commissioners shall issue their order to the trustees of the proper township or
townships,* directing the road to be opened."

10. Having received such notice, he should then notify the persons having control of the land over which such road extends, to remove the fences from the ground such road will occupy. He should do this chiefly to give them a chance to protect their crops, etc., on and near the line of said road, especially if it must be opened before such crops have ripened and been removed.

11. Should such persons unreasonably delay to comply with his notice, it is then his duty to proceed to so remove them himself, and to improve such road by removing the necessary trees, etc., by grading and otherwise working said road as much as necessary or possible, having due regard to the claims and needs of other roads in his district.

12. The notice by the supervisor, mentioned above, may be oral, or in writing, in some such form as follows:

To C—— D——: You are hereby notified that a new township road has been duly established, which passes through my district and through your land, as follows [*here describe the line of the road through C—— D——'s land.*]

You are requested and required to remove all fences and buildings on your land standing on the line of said road, before the —— day of ——, 18—.

A—— B——, Supervisor.

13. If the road is narrowed, the adjoining land-owner may set his fences out to the new line; and if the road is ordered to be widened, the supervisor may, after being duly notified thereof by the township clerk, cause the fences to be set back to the new line by the owner, and on such owner's failure to do so, the supervisor may remove them as he would any other obstruction, being careful not unnecessarily to damage or destroy the materials composing such fences. He is simply to *remove*, not to *rebuild*, the fences.

14. *Unlawful ditches along road.* It is unlawful for any supervisor to excavate or make any open ditch on and along a public highway in front of any dwelling house or yard surrounding it, or entrance thereto, or in front of the entrance or approach to any barn on that side of the road on which the said buildings are situate, unless he at once puts in a sufficient underdrain, and fills up the excavation to the original level; except when authorized to make such open ditch at said points, by the owner of such buildings or trustees of the township. Any road supervisor violating this paragraph is liable to forfeit and pay to the owner of any such buildings twenty-five dollars, to be recovered in a civil action before any justice of the peace. (§ 4715a, 89 O. L. 41.)

15. *Certain ditches must be kept open.* The law provides

how certain land owners may construct underground out-
let drains through the land of another, and that the ditches
and water-courses upon the highways into which such
underground drains empty, shall be kept open by the supervisor of such public highways, to a depth sufficient for
the proper drainage of such highways. (88 O. L. 350.)

16. *Supervisor must repair roads, and remove obstructions.*
The law provides that every supervisor must keep in repair all public roads and highways which are laid out and
established in his road district, and remove, or cause to be
removed, all encroachments, by fences or otherwise, and
all obstructions that may from time to time be found
thereon.[1] (4715, as am. 86 v. 231.)

(1) Wnere there has been a continued use of a highway, although its
width had been encroached upon by the adjacent owner for eighteen years,
the right is not lost. The supervisor may open such road to its full width.
Fox *v.* Hart, 11 Ohio, 414.

A supervisor is a local ministerial officer, whose authority and duties to
open, repair, and control public roads, extends only to the roads within
his own district. Grove *v.* Mikesell, 13 Ohio St. 153.

Where a highway, sixty feet in width, is established across a stream of
water, and a bridge twelve feet wide is constructed along the center of such
highway over the stream, and a proprietor of adjoining lands constructs
fences from the outer limits of the road, along the bank of the stream, to
the bridge: *Held,* that such fences are, *prima facie,* at least, obstructions
of the highway, and as such it is the duty of the supervisor of the proper
district, on due notice, and doing no unnecessary damage, to remove them;
and for so doing, an action for trespass will not lie against him. Baird *v.*
Clark, 12 Ohio, 87.

L. being the owner of lands adjoining a public highway, regularly laid
out and used by the public, extended his fence so as to inclose a portion of
the ground within the surveyed lines of the highway, which portion was
not then used nor required for the public travel, and kept up said fence
without any objection for upward of twenty-one years: *Held,* that such
partial encroachment upon the side of a surveyed and traveled highway
was not *necessarily adverse* to the public, nor *inconsistent* with its ease-
ment, and therefore constituted no bar to its reclamation by the supervisor, when required for the public travel. Lane *v.* Kennedy et al., 13 Ohio
St. 42.

No penalty is given for obstructing a road authorized by law, nor for permitting the obstruction to remain, unless it is to the *hinderance or inconvenience* of travelers, and therefore the defendant may show that travelers
were not accustomed to pass the state road obstructed by him, but that the
travel was on a turnpike road, shorter and more convenient. Ingersoll *v.*
Herider, 12 Ohio, 527.

The right of transit in the use of the public highways is subject to such
incidental, temporary, or partial obstructions as manifest necessity requires; and among these are the temporary impediments necessarily occasioned in the building and repair of houses on lots fronting upon the streets
of a city, and in the construction of sewers, drains, etc. These are not in-
vasions, but qualifications of the right of transit on the public highway;
and the limitation on them is, that they must not be unnecessarily and unreasonably interposed. Clark *v.* Fry, 8 Ohio St. 358.

As fuel is necessary, a man may throw wood into the street for the purpose of having it carried into his house, and it may lie there a reasonable
time. Ib.

Where a road has been laid out in the manner prescribed by law, opened
and used for many years, it can not be allowed that it shall be suddenly
closed by any individual through whose land it passes, on the hypothesis
that the road used does not exactly follow the courses and distances of the
recorded survey. Nor can it be required, after the lapse of many years,
that to sustain a public road, every preliminary step necessary to be taken
to establish it, must be proven by existing papers or records. Arnold *v.*
Flattery, 5 Ohio, 79.

17. *Obstructions to be removed.* At any time during the year when any public highway is obstructed, the supervisor of the district must forthwith cauze the obstruction to be removed, for which purpose he must immediately order out such number of persons liable to do work or pay tax upon the public highways of his district as he may deem necessary; if any person thus called out has performed his two days' labor upon the pub'ic highways, or paid his road tax, the supervisor must give him a certificate for the amount of labor performed under such order, which may be applied on the labor or tax that may be due from such person the next year. (4746.)

18. The order may be verbal, or written or printed, and may be in form as follows:

Road District No. ——, —— Tp., —— Co., O.
—— ——, 18—.

To ——:

You are hereby notified to appear on the —— day of ——, 18—, at 7 o'clock forenoon, at ——, to assist in removing certain obstructions there on the public highway. The labor then done by you will be credited as a part of the two days' labor required of you by law, for the year 18—. You will bring with you the following implements: (*name the implements.*)   —— ——, Supervisor.

19. The certificate must be written or printed, and may be as follows:

Road District No. ——, —— Tp., —— Co., O.
—— ——, 18—.

I hereby certify that R—— L—— has performed (*one half, or more, as may be*) day's extra labor on the roads of said district in said year, for which he is entitled to credit on any road labor required of him by law during the year 18—.   A—— B——,
Supervisor of said District.

20. *Only public roads to be worked.* A supervisor must not

A supervisor can not begin and conduct, in his own name, a suit for an injunction to prevent the obstruction of a public road. Putnam v. Valentine, 5 Ohio, 187.

Where, in an action before a justice (for obstructing the road), the plaintiff was described as " A. B., supervisor of road district No. 6, Stonecreek township, Clermont county," on appeal, the supervisor for the time being may file his petition as "supervisor of road district No. 6," etc. Hill v. Supervisor, 10 Ohio St. 621.

Where private lands are erroneously included in a road by review and survey, the supervisor is liable in trespass for entering upon the land and digging up the soil; and he is not protected by the record of the survey and the declaration of the statute that the road as surveyed shall be considered a public highway. Beckwith v. Beckwith. 22 Ohio St. 180.

A supervisor is not liable for damages to an individual for injuries that individual has sustained because of the neglect of the supervisor to keep a bridge within his district in repair. The supervisor is liable only for the penalty prescribed by law. Dunlap v. Knapp, 14 Ohio St. 64. (As to what this penalty is, see paragraph 84, this chapter.) See also note 1, page 5, and note 1, page 25, paragraph 76.

perform nor cause to be performed labor on any road not regularly laid out and established by-law. (4743.)

21. *May enter lands for trees, gravel, etc.* Supervisors may enter upon any uncultivated or improved lands unincumbered by crops, near to or adjoining such roads, cut and carry away timber,[1] except trees or groves on improved lands, planted or left for ornament or shade, and may dig, or cause to be dug and carried away, any gravel, sand, or stone which may be necessary to make, improve, or repair any such road.[1] (4715, as am. 86 v. 231.)

22. *Certificate for timber, etc., taken for road.* A supervisor of roads, or a superintendent of a free turnpike, improved, or other macadamized road having no gate thereon, who takes any timber, stone, or gravel for the purpose of making, improving, or repairing any road or structure, or repairing any bridge or crossway within his district, must, on demand of the owner of the land, or his agent, or the guardian of any ward, or the executor of any will, having the lands in charge from which the same were taken, give a certificate[2] showing the quantity of such timber, stone, or gravel, with the value thereof respectively, and the time and purpose for which the same was taken. (4744, 4715, as am. 86 v. 231.)

23. The certificate may be as follows:

Road District No. ——, —— Tp., —— Co., O.
—— ——, 18—.

I hereby certify that in making [*or* improving, *or* repairing] the county [*or* state, *or* township] road leading from —— to —— [*or* bridge, *giving its name or location*], within said district, on the —— day of ——, 18—, I took from the land of L—— M——, the following materials for the purpose of said improvement, as follows:

1 large oak tree, worth		$7 00
1 locust tree,	"	1 00
10 loads gravel,	"	2 00
3 perch of stone,	"	1 50

Total.............................$11 50
A—— B——, Supervisor.

[1] § 4715 was unconstitutional, but has been amended to cure this. See 44 O. S. 208; 86 O. L. 231.
When a supervisor, entering to cut timber for repairing a road, commits waste, he becomes a trespasser from the beginning. Palmer *v.* State, Wright, 364.
The authority to cut timber to repair roads includes authority to cut for the purpose of repairing a bridge on a road. This power is operative whenever the road, etc., is out of repair. Ib.
The owner of the material so taken is entitled to compensation therefor, to be assessed by the trustees, and paid as specified in section 4745 (4715, as am. 86 v. 231). See next note.
(2) A person who receives such certificate must present the same to the township trustees of the proper township, at any regular or called session, within twelve months after the taking of such timber, stone, or gravel, and the trustees, if satisfied that the amount is just and equitable, must pay the same. See more fully § 4745.

24. *May enter lands to make ditches, etc.* A supervisor may also enter upon any lands adjoining or lying near the road, and make such drains or ditches through the same as he may deem necessary for the benefit of the road ; but he must do as little injury to such lands, and the improvements and timber thereon, as the nature of the case and the public good will permit ; the drains and ditches so made must be conducted to the nearest water-course, and must be kept open by the supervisor ; and they must not be obstructed by the owner or occupier of the lands, or any other person having the same in charge, under a penalty not exceeding ten dollars for each offense, which must be collected by the supervisor, and paid by him to the township treasurer, and applied to the road fund of the township. (4716.)

25. *Two days' work on roads.* Formerly, all male persons between 21 and 55 years of age, with certain exceptions, had to work two days on the public roads, under the direction of the supervisor ; but all laws requiring this two days' work have been repealed.[1]

26. *Road taxes may be worked out,* under the supervisor's direction. See pars. 46–48, 54–57, and others, this chapter.

27. *Trustees to furnish plows and scrapers.* The township trustees are authorized to furnish plows and scrapers for the use of the several road districts within their township, to be paid for out of any money in the township treasury not otherwise appropriated. They must take a receipt from each supervisor for such implements as they deliver to him, showing the number, kind, and condition thereof ; and such supervisor will be liable for any injury or damage that may result to such implements, or any of them, by the improper use thereof, or by unnecessary exposure to the weather during the time the same may be in his possession, to be recovered in an action in the name of the trustees. On the first Monday in March, annually, he must return these implements to the trustees. (4735.)

28–41. The supervisor's receipt may be as follows :

NO.	NAMES OF ARTICLES.	CONDITION.
1	Road plow..................................	Nearly new.
1	Scraper....................................	New.
1	Scraper....................................	Much worn.
10	Shovels..................................	Worn.
	Etc.	

Received the articles above mentioned from the township trustees, this —— day of ——, 18—.   A—— B——, Supervisor.

(1) See act of 91 O. L. 342, repealing sections 2658, 2659, 2653, 4717, 4718, 4719, 4720, 4721, 4722, 4723, 4724, 4725, 4726, 4727 and 4728.
A few provisions concerning such work, probably overlooked, still remain. See, for instance, pars. 17, 70, 85, this chapter ; pars. 14, 20, chap. 3.

42. *Road beds to be leveled off.* Every supervisor must cause to be graded and leveled off, the earth and gravel that may be scraped, shoveled, or hauled into any public road under his direction or charge, at the time that such work is performed; and for any neglect or refusal, on the part of such supervisor, to cause such leveling or grading in a reasonable degree, he will forfeit not less than one dollar nor more than five dollars, to be paid into the township road fund, to be recovered by an action in the name of the township, before a justice of the peace within the township where such supervisor resides; and the trustees of the township, after having been notified by any resident freeholder of the township of such neglect or refusal, must, by one of their number, examine the work, and if he find that it has not been performed, in a reasonable degree, according to the provisions of this section, he must prosecute such supervisor as provided herein. (4729.)

43. *Roads on state or township lines.* A supervisor of a road district bordering on the state line between Ohio and an adjoining state may, when a public highway has been located upon such state line in accordance with and under the provisions of the laws of the State of Ohio, apply the labor of his district upon such road in the same manner as on roads located within the boundaries of the state. (4747.)

44. In case any public road is or may be established as a ' part of the line or boundary of any township or municipal corporation, the trustees of such adjoining townships, and council of such corporation, as the case may be, must meet at some convenient place as soon after the first Monday of March as convenient, and apportion such road between the townships, or township and corporations, as justice and equity may require, and the trustees of the respective townships, and council of the corporation must have the road opened and improved accordingly. (4747.)

45. *Additional road tax for cutting down hills, etc.* If township trustees deem an additional road tax necessary, they must determine the per centum to be levied upon the taxable property of their respective townships, not exceeding three mills on the dollar; for the purpose of cutting down hills, filling low places, and making repairs that may be necessary by reason of any casualty that may occur in the public highways of their respective townships, which must not, in any year, exceed the sum of two hundred dollars, unless the question of a greater levy be submitted to a vote of the qualified voters of the township, at a special election called by the trustees for that purpose; if a majority of the qualified voters at such election vote in favor of levying an increased tax, for the purposes aforesaid, the trustees must certify the same to the county auditor, in

writing, on or before the first Monday of June in each
year, and the auditor must assess the same on the taxable
property in the township, not included in any municipal
corporation, and the same must be collected in the December installment, and paid out as other taxes, except as
hereinafter provided.[1] (4737.)

46. *Rate of such levy to be published.* The auditor of each
county, immediately after the county commissioners and
trustees of townships, at their annual sessions for that
purpose, have determined the amounts to be assessed for
road purposes in their respective counties and townships,
must give notice, in some newspaper in general circulation
in the county, of the per centum on each hundred dollars
of the valuation so determined to be assessed in such
county and township respectively, and that said tax may
be discharged by labor on the roads, under the direction
of the supervisors of the several districts; and he must
make a list of the names of tax payers, and the amount
of the road tax with which each stands charged, and
transmit the same to the clerk of the proper township.
(4738.)

47. *Tax to be certified to supervisors.* The township clerk,
immediately after the receipt of such list, must make out
and deliver to each supervisor an abstract of the amount
of road tax each person in his district is charged with.
(4739.)

48. *How road tax worked out or paid, etc.* Any person
charged with a road tax may discharge the same by labor
on the public highways, within the proper time, at the
rate of one dollar and fifty cents per day, and a ratable
allowance per day for any team and implements furnished
by any person, under the direction of the supervisor of
the proper district, who must give to such person a certificate specifying the amount of tax so paid, and the district

(1) Section 2829, from the title on taxation (Part First, Title XIII), is very
much like the law in this paragraph. It is as follows:
"SEC. 2829 *Additional road tax.* If the trustees of any township shall
deem an additional road tax necessary, they shall determine the per
centum to be levied on the taxable property of their township, not exceeding one mill on the dollar, except in counties where the taxable property
is less than ten millions, in which counties the trustees of the different
townships thereof may, at their discretion, levy an additional road tax,
not to exceed two mills on the dollar valuation of the taxable property of
their township; which may be discharged in labor as hereinafter provided, and in addition thereto not exceeding one mill on the dollar for the
same purpose to be collected in money; but where a township shall include
an incorporated village, the rate of tax so fixed by said township trustees
shall not apply, or be assessed or collected from the property included
within the incorporated limits of such village; but the council of any such
village shall exercise the right conferred by this title on the trustees of
townships to make such additional levy, for road purposes, on the taxable
property within the corporate limits of any such village, as trustees may,
by this title, make for road purposes in their respective townships; and
said trustees and council shall certify the same to the county auditor, in
writing, on or before the fifteenth day of May each year; and the auditor
of the county shall assess the same on all the taxable property in the said
township or village, and the same shall be collected in the December installment."

and township wherein such labor was performed. This
certificate must in no case be given for any greater sum
than the tax charged against such person; and the county
treasurer must receive all such certificates as money in the
discharge of said road tax. When the commissioners of
any county _so direct, the supervisor must write on the
margin of his lists, opposite to the amount charged against
all such as may pay the same by money or labor, the word
"paid," and must return his list to the township clerk on
or before the fifth day of September of the year in which
the tax was levied. The clerk must then write on the
margin of the list sent him by the auditor, opposite to the
amount charged against each person who may have paid
the same in labor or money, as shown by the returns of
the supervisor, the word "paid," and must forthwith for-
ward the same to the county auditor, who must charge all
such as may remain unpaid, as shown by the returns of
the township clerk, upon the duplicate of the proper
county, and the same must be collected as other moneys
are collected, in the December installment, by the county
treasurer. When such road tax is paid in labor, such labor
must be performed before the first day of September of
the year in which levied. (2830, as amended, 77 O. L. 184.)

49. *Certain exceptions to this.* In all counties containing either graveled roads or free turnpikes, or both, except Shelby and Allen counties, the time for the payment of the road tax in labor on such roads
may extend to the fifteenth of October of the year the tax was levied;
but on all other roads in such counties the labor must be performed
before the fifteenth of September; and the supervisors in such counties must return their lists before the twenty-fifth of October of the
year in which the tax was levied. (2830, as amended.) See also par.
2, chap. 4, of this book.

50. *Form of certificate.* I hereby certify that R—— L—— has paid in
labor —— dollars and —— cents, being in full [or, *if not paid in full,*
say, on account] of his road tax for the year 18—, in road district
No. ——, —— township, —— county, Ohio, and that such labor was
performed between the —— day of —— and —— day of ——, 18—.
—— ——, 18—   —— ——, Supervisor.

51. *Extra road tax for improving certain roads.* When
two-thirds of the resident freehold tax-payers living on
the line of any state road, county road, or turnpike road,
file a petition with the auditor of any county for an extra
tax for the purpose of constructing, improving, or repairing such road, he must levy such tax, of any amount that
may be required, not exceeding six mills on the dollar
valuation, in any year, on all the lands and taxable property for any distance on each side of such road not exceeding one mile, and in no case more than half the distance from such road to any other state, county, or free
turnpike road running parallel or nearly parallel thereto.
(4925.)

52. *How long such tax to continue.* When any such tax is

levied, it must continue for the term of three years and
no longer, unless at the expiration of three years the petition or request be renewed; and in that event such tax
may be levied for the term of three years longer. (4926.)

53. *When such tax may be levied in a township.* The auditor
of any county must levy such tax on the lands and property on the line of any such road, in any township, when
petitioned for by three-fourths of the resident freehold
tax-payers on such road, in such township only. (4927.)

54. *Such tax may be repaid in labor, under supervisor's direc-
tions.* All taxes arising under the provisions of the three
preceding paragraphs may be discharged by labor on the
proper road, under the direction of the supervisors within
whose jurisdiction such road is located, as provided by
law in other cases; and the rate of labor shall be one dollar and fifty cents per day, and a ratable proportion for
teams and implements. (4928.)

55. *Supervisor to give receipts.* If such taxes be discharged
by labor, the supervisors must receipt therefor, as in other
cases for like services, and their receipts must be received
by the county treasurer in discharge of such tax. (4929.)

56. The form of receipt is the same as given in paragraph 50.

57. The trustees of any township may, upon the written
petition of one or more persons interested, describing the
road or part thereof proposed to be improved, authorize
any person living on or near any unimproved state,
county, or township road, situate within the township,
which intersects or connects with any turnpike or improved road, to improve any part or all of such road situate within the township, within such time as they may
direct, by grading the same not more than sixteen feet
wide, and graveling such grade not exceeding twelve feet
wide, or otherwise improving the same; such improvement must be made under the instructions of the supervisors of roads within whose districts the road or part
thereof to be improved is situate; and as soon as such
road or part thereof authorized to be improved as aforesaid, within any road district, is fully improved and completed to the satisfaction of the supervisor of such district,
he must estimate the work so done by the several persons
authorized, either by themselves or those employed by
them, under such rules and regulations as the township
trustees must prescribe as to extent and character of such
improvement, and give to such persons a certificate specifying the amount of labor performed by them, stating
when authority was given to improve such road, and when
the same was completed in his district, and accepted by
him, and the value in money of such labor so estimated;
but in estimating the value of such labor in money, the

supervisor must not allow a greater sum than two dollars and twenty-five cents for each team and driver, and not to exceed one dollar for each hand per day for the time actually employed; and in case of dispute between the supervisor, and any person interested in such improvement, as to the manner of making the same, its completion, or the value of the work, the matter in dispute must be submitted to the trustees of the township, and their decision will be final. (4755.)

58. The certificate mentioned above may be in the following form:

Road District No. ——, —— Tp., —— Co., O.

—— ——, 18—.

I hereby certify that L—— O—— has performed labor on the [*here name or otherwise describe the road*] road within said district, between the —— day of ——, 18—, and the —— day of ——, 18—, the prices set forth being allowed by me, as follows:

One [*or more, as may be,*] hand, for —— days, at ——

per day... $——

One [*or more, as may be,*] team, for —— days, at ——-

per day............ ——

The authority to improve said road was given on the —— day of ——, 18—, and the improvement was completed in said district on the —— day of ——, 18—, and accepted by me on the —— day of ——, 18—.

A—— B——, Supervisor.

59. The holder of any such certificate will be entitled to have its amount credited on any road tax, payable in labor, levied on the property of such person situate within the county, after the completion of such improvement; if such road tax levied in any year on such property is not sufficient to cover the amount of the certificate, it must be so credited from year to year, until the certificate is fully paid without interest. At the time of making such credit upon the certificate, the supervisor must give to the owner of the certificate a receipt for the road tax charged against him for the current year; and the owner of the certificate may transfer it, or any balance due on it, to any subsequent purchaser of the property owned by him when the certificate was issued. (4756.)

60. The receipt may be in form as follows:

Road District No. ——, —— Tp., —— Co., O.

—— ——, 18—.

The road tax charged against L—— O——, in said district, for the year 18—, has been paid to the extent of —— dollars and —— cents, by labor done in said district in the year 18—, and described in his certificate therefor, dated

—— ——, 18—, and signed by A—— B——, supervisor. I have this day credited said amount as paid on said certificate.   C—— D——, Supervisor.

At the same time the foregoing receipt is given, the following or its equivalent must be indorsed on such certificate:

On this —— day of ——, 18—, I have given to L—— O——, a receipt for road tax for this year, to the extent of —— dollars and —— cents, on account of the within certificate.   C—— D——,
Supervisor of within named District.

61. The trustees, at the time of authorizing such improvement, must direct in their order at what point the materials therefor shall be taken, under the general laws in force for procuring materials for the improvement of public roads, which point must be the nearest and most convenient to the place where the materials can be procured in the township. But where a road is located in two townships, the material for the improvement thereof may be procured at the nearest and most convenient point in either township. (4757.)

62. *Drift against bridges and culverts, in ditches, etc., to be removed.* The supervisor of each road district, or the superintendent of any free turnpike or improved road, must remove, or cause to be removed, all timber or drift lodged against bridges, except toll bridges or bridges upon toll roads; and all timber, drift, and sediment lodged in and obstructing the free passage of water in ditches constructed for the draining and protection of such roads, or under or against any culvert over the same, or over any natural water-course adjoining and upon the line of free turnpikes, and all other public roads in his district. He will receive the same compensation for such work or duties performed as is prescribed by law for other road work. (4731, as am. 86 v. 28.)

63. *Penalty.* In case any supervisor or superintendent fails or neglects to comply with the provisions of this paragraph, he will be liable to a fine of not less than five and not more than twenty-five dollars. Any adjoining landowner affected thereby may, at the expiration of ten days, after serving a written notice on such supervisor or superintendent to remove any such drift or sediment, remove or cause the same to be removed; for which he will receive the same compensation and from the same source as such supervisor or superintendent would have been entitled to in the performance of his duty. (4731, as am. 86 v. 28.)

64. *Sidewalks, foot-bridges, etc., along road.* The supervisor, when authorized by the trustees, may construct on either side of any public road in his district a public foot-walk, sidewalk, or foot-bridge over streams of water, of such material and at such expense as the trustees shall prescribe,

which must not in any manner obstruct the public highway, or any private entrance; or the trustees may construct, by contract with the lowest responsible bidder; all such improvements to be paid for out of the township road funds. (4733, as am. 78 v. 84.)

65. *Passways may be constructed.* Any landholder through whose land a state, county, or township road is now or may be hereafter laid out and established, is authorized, under the direction of the supervisor of the proper district, to construct a passway either over or under such road, so as to permit stock to pass and repass; but the passway must not be constructed over or under any road within the limits of the outlots of a city, town, or village, and must not hinder or obstruct the travel on such roads, and must be kept in good repair at the expense of the landholder. (4740.)

66. *Weeds, bushes, briers, etc., in road to be cut down.* Road superintendents, and supervisors, and street commissioners, must, between June 15th and 30th, and between August 1st and 15th, and between September 15th and 30th, of each year, cut all brush, briers, Canada or common thistles, or any other noxious weeds growing within the limits of any county or township road, or improved road, street, or alley, within their jurisdiction. Such superintendent or supervisor may allow any landowner or tenant to cut and destroy any such brush, briers, or weeds, growing on such highway along the lands abutting thereon owned or occupied by such landowner or tenant, fixing a reasonable compensation for such work before it is done. Such compensation must be credited on the road tax of that year assessed against said premises. Such superintendent or supervisor must, by the township trustees, be allowed $1.50 per day for all such necessary labor, to be paid by the township treasurer out of the road fund, then in his hands. Superintendents of toll roads must do likewise as to such weeds, etc., growing along their turnpikes, at said times, or the township trustees must have it done, and collect pay and penalty therefor before any justice of the peace in the township. (4730, as am., 90 O. L. 301.)

67. *Canada thistles to be destroyed.* It was formerly the duty of the supervisor of any road district, when notified in writing that any Canada thistles were about to go to seed on *any land* within his district, to cause the same to be destroyed in time to prevent the seed from spreading. But this duty, is now imposed on the township trustees.[1] He must still destroy them along the road. See par. 66.

68. *Obstruction of roads by railroad agents and other persons.* If any person or corporation, or a conductor of any train

(1) See § 4732, as am., 90 O. L. 302. As to brush or thistles along partition fences, etc., see §§ [4255,-1]-[4255,-5], 7001, of Giauque's edition of the Revised Statutes.

of railroad cars, or any other agent or servant of a railroad company, obstruct, unnecessarily, any public road or highway authorized by any law of this state, by permitting any railroad car or locomotive to remain upon or across the same for a longer period than five minutes, or permit any timber, lumber, wood, or other obstruction to remain upon or across the same to the hinderance or inconvenience of travelers, or any person passing along or upon such road or highway, every person or corporation so offending shall forfeit and pay, for every such offense, any sum not exceeding twenty nor less than two dollars, and will be liable for all damages arising to any person from such obstruction, or injury to such road or highway, to be recovered by an action at the suit of the trustees of the township in which the offense is committed, or of any person suing for the same before a justice of the peace within the county where the offense is committed, or by indictment in the court of common pleas in the proper county;[1] every twenty-four hours such person or corporation, after being notified, suffers such obstruction to remain, must be deemed an additional offense against the provisions of this paragraph; and all fines accruing under this paragraph, when collected, must be paid to the treasurer of the township in which the offense was committed, and be applied by the trustees to the improvement of roads and highways therein. (4748.)

69. *Company liable for fines against employes.* Every railroad company or other corporation, the servant, agent, or

(1) By section 32 of the act relating to roads (S. & S. 609), township trustees are authorized to bring civil actions to recover the statutory penalty for obstructing and permitting obstructions to remain upon and across public roads or highways authorized by the laws of this state, to the hinderance and inconvenience of travelers or other persons passing along or upon such public roads or highways. Trust es of Burton Township *v.* Tuttle et a'., 30 Ohio St. 62.

The statute giving the cause of action confers jurisdiction over it upon justices of the peace. Ib.

In actions prosecuted und r the provisions of this statute, where the obstruction is alleged to have been caused by a railroad car, or cars, or locomotive, it must be averred in the petition that the public road or highway was obstructed unnecessarily, by permitting such railroad car or cars, or locomotive, to remain upon or across t'e public road or highway for a longer period than five minutes, to the hinderance, etc. In actions for obstructions to public roads caused by agencies other than railroad cars and locomotives, in describing he manner of the obstruction, the word "*unnecessarily*" forms no essential part of the description of the cause of action. Ib.

It is no valid objection to the jurisdiction of a justice of the peace in this class of cases, that, on the trial, the right of the public to the use of the roadway, as a public highway. may involve, to some extent, the title to the land at the place of alleged obstruction. As the statute confers original jurisdiction upon justices of the peace over the cause of action, by necessary implication it vests authority in justices' courts to hear and determine all questions necessary to render a final judgment. Ib.

The person who maintains a mill-race, divering water from its natural flow through the race to his mill, for private u e, which mill race cuts and crosses a public r ad previously established over his land by authority of law, which race unbridged is an obstruction across the highway, to the hinderance and inconvenience of travelers and persons going along and upon such public highway, must place a sufficient bridge over the race at the point of obstruction, and keep it in repair so that the highway will be as good and safe for public travel as before the race was constructed. Ic.

employe of which, in any manner, obstructs any public road or highway, will be liable to pay all fines which may be assessed against such servant, agent, or employe for so obstructing the same, and such liability may be enforced by execution issued against such corporation on the judgment rendered against such servant, agent, or employe. (4749.)

70. *How fires in woods or prairies extinguished.* Whenever the woods or prairies in any township are on fire, so as seriously to endanger property, the trustees of such township may order as many of the inhabitants of the township, liable to work on the highways, and residents in the vicinity of the place where such fire is, as they may deem necessary, to repair to the place where such fire is, and there to assist in extinguishing the same, or stopping its progress; and every person called out, under the provision of this section, must be allowed, by the supervisor of his road district, to be applied on his poll or road tax, the same amount per day that he is now allowed for work on public highways. (4750.)

71. *Penalties for refusal to assist.* If a person refuse or willfully neglect to comply with such order, he shall forfeit a sum not less than five nor more than fifty dollars, to be collected before any justice of the peace of the township. (4751.)

72. The following certificate may be given:

Road District, No. ——, —— Township, —— County, O.
                                                 ——, 18—.

I certify that E—— F—— has been, by me, ordered out to assist in extinguishing fires in the woods (*or*, prairies, *as may be*), in said district; that he was thus employed for one-half day, for which he is entitled to seventy-five cents, to be credited to any road or poll tax against him now due or to become due.   A—— B——, Supervisor.

73. *Bridges over mill-races, etc.* No person possessed of the right to any water privilege is required by law to build, nor keep in repair, and bridge over any mill-race or watercourse constructed by such person across any public road for hydraulic purposes.[1] (4752.)

74. When any road is hereafter established, the owner of such right must file in the county auditor's office, within a year after such road is established, a written declaration of such right, describing and stating as near as practicable, where he intends some time to excavate a mill-race or water-course across the road. This declaration must be recorded by the auditor, and will secure such right to the owner, his heirs, and assigns. But nothing in this section can prevent such owner from constructing a mill-race or water-course across any public

(1) See last paragraph of note, page 23.

highway already established, on giving the notice required
in the next paragraph. (4753.)

75. *Duty of supervisor in certain cases.* When any person
excavates or constructs a mill-race across a public highway, he must give at least thirty days previous notice,
in writing, to the trustees of the proper township, of his
intention so to do; and if he fail or neglect to give such
notice, the supervisor of the proper road district may, if
in his opinion the public good demands it, fill up such
mill-race or water-course, at the cost of the party so failing
and neglecting to give notice, to be recovered by the supervisor, together with fifty per centum thereon, and the
costs of suit, for the use of such road district, in an action
before any court of competent jurisdiction.[1] (4754.)

76. *Supervisor must settle with township trustees, when.* At
the annual March meeting of the township trustees, they
must settle the accounts of the supervisors; and for this
purpose the supervisors must attend that meeting. (1458,
as am., 90 O. L. 98.)

77. *Supervisor's report to trustees.* The supervisor should
render to the township trustees at this meeting an account
of his receipts and expenditures, and of his work, etc.,
arranged under suitable heads or parts. Without it, a
proper settlement can scarcely be made at all. To aid in
making such report, and to secure uniformity, the trustees
should furnish him with suitable blanks therefor.

78. *The form of such report* may be substantially as follows :

SUPERVISOR'S REPORT AND SETTLEMENT.

79.   [First.]

Statement of moneys received by me as supervisor.

Amount received from [*state whom—see pars.* 24, 75].	$10 25
Total cash road tax collected, as shown by "Abstract of Road Tax" returned to clerk on —— —, 18—..	89 50
Amount of road tax received from township trustees.	25 00
Collected by suit from [*state whom—see pars.* 24, 75].	7 50
Etc., etc...................................	
Total receipts.............................	$132 25

---

(1) But he can not be held personally liable for the payment of costs
in such cases. See paragraph 3, and Bittle *v.* Hay, 5 Ohio, 269.
  An action for obstructing a highway should be brought, not in the
name of the supervisor (*individually*), but the plaintiff should be supervisor of road district No. ——, in township ——, of —— county. .
Hill *v.* Supervisor, 10 Ohio St. 622.
  Where, in an action before a justice of the peace, the plaintiff was
described as A. B., supervisor of road district No. 6, Stonecreek, Clermont county, on appeal, the supervisor for the time being may file his
petition as "The Supervisor of Road District No. 6," etc. Ib.

80.   [Second.]

Statement of moneys expended by me as supervisor.

[Give the items of all moneys expended. It is sup-
posed, *of course*, that the supervisor has taken a receipt
for every cent expended. These receipts should be numbered in the order of their dates, and are, in this settlement, the supervisor's vouchers for the truth of his state-
ments as to expended money.]

TO WHOM PAID AND WHAT FOR.	No. of Voucher.	Amount
....	....	....
....	....	....
....	....	....
....	....	....
....	....	....
....	....	....
....	....	....
....	....	....
Total expenditures		$128 75

Total received $132 25
Total expended 128 75

Balance on hand............................ $3 50

81.   [Third.]

Statement of my personal account.

I was employed in the discharge of my official duties,
as follows:
Superintending labor.. ... days.
Attending suits ....   "
Etc., etc ....   "
Etc., etc ....   "

Total .... 20 days.
Due me, at $1.50 per day, $30.
For which I ask an appropriation.

I certify the foregoing to be a correct report of my proceedings, and a true statement of my receipts and expenditures, during my term of office as supervisor since
my election in April last.

A—— B——, Supervisor.

82. *Receipt for road implements returned to trustees.* The
supervisor should then get a receipt from the trustees for

the plows, scrapers, etc., which he returns to them as required of him by paragraph 25.

83. *The form of this receipt* may be as follows:

NO.	NAMES OF ARTICLES.	CONDITION.
1	Road plow...............................	Nearly new.
1	Scraper................................	New.
1	Scraper................................	Much worn.
10	Shovels...............................	Worn.
	Etc.	

Received the articles above mentioned from A——
B——, supervisor of road district No. ——, this —— day
of ——, 18—.

> J—— C——,
> C—— S——,
> O—— P——,
> Township Trustees.

84. *Penalties against supervisors.* A supervisor who neglects or refuses to perform the several duties enjoined on him by this chapter, or who, under any pretense whatever, gives or signs any receipt or certificate, purporting to be a receipt or certificate for labor or work performed, or money paid, unless the labor shall have been performed or money paid before the giving or signing of such receipt or certificate, will forfeit, for every such offense, not less than five dollars nor more than fifty dollars, to be recovered in an action before a justice of the peace within the township where he resides; and the trustees of the township must prosecute all offenses against the provisions of this paragraph; but if a supervisor conceives himself aggrieved by the judgment of such justice, he may, on giving sufficient security for the payment of costs, appeal to the court of common pleas; which must make such order therein as to it may appear just and reasonable. (4742.) See also paragraph 63, chapter 2, and paragraphs 23 and 24 of chapter 4.

85. *Compensation.* Every supervisor must be paid for his services, not more than one dollar and fifty cents per day, for the time he is actually employed on the roads; but no supervisor can be allowed, in any one year, more than twelve dollars, in addition to the remuneration for his two days' labor on the roads, when the number of persons in his district, liable to work on the roads, does not exceed twenty-five; not more than sixteen dollars, when the number so liable is more than twenty-five and less than thirty-five; not more than twenty-five dollars, when the

number so liable is not less than thirty-five nor more than fifty; and not more than thirty-five dollars, when the number so liable exceeds fifty; but a supervisor that is required, by any law of the state, to repair a turnpike road, or any part thereof, must be allowed not exceeding eight per cent. for the amount of the labor performed under his direction as supervisor, repairing such turnpike or working out the road tax in his district; but in no case shall he receive more than one dollar and fifty cents per day. (1533).

CHAPTER III.

RELATING TO FREE TURNPIKES.

1. REPAIRS OF IMPROVED ROADS.

1. *What are "improved roads"—How repaired.* All macadamized roads which are free roads, whether constructed under general or local laws by taxation or assessment, or both, or converted by purchase or otherwise from a toll road into a free road under any law, and all turnpike roads, or parts thereof, unfinished or abandoned by any turnpike company, and appropriated or accepted by the commissioners of the county, must be kept in repair as is provided in this chapter. (4876.)

2. The greater part of the duties relating to such repairs fall upon officers other than supervisors, as will be seen by this chapter. But it will also be seen that supervisors are, or may be, also charged with certain duties in relation to these repairs, and therefore so much of the law relating to this subject as may be useful to supervisors, for the purpose of showing them what duties *are not* theirs, and what others *are* or *may become* theirs, is here given.

SPECIAL PROVISIONS FOR CERTAIN COUNTIES.

3. *In certain counties.* Formerly, in Darke, Logan, Clermont, and Shelby counties, improved roads were under the charge and control of officers entitled pike superintendents, and with them supervisors had nothing to do, except that the township trustees set off certain persons. who had to perform their two days' labor, and their labor in commutation of taxes, under the direction of these superintendents. The supervisor could not order nor compel such persons to labor under him. The township trustees had to give these superintendents the use of the township plows, scrapers, and other road implements. Some understanding was therefore necessary, through the township clerk and trustees, what persons were so set off, and when those implements could be used by the supervisor, and when by the superintendents, in such road dis-. tricts where both these officers had work to do. See §§ 4877–4888. But by changes in the law,[1] no counties are now in this class.

4. *In certain other counties.* The law makes each town-

(1) Including the repeal of §4877, in 91 O. L. 183; see old §4877; note to par. 3, chapter 10, of Giauque's " Road and Bridge Laws."

ship in the counties of Belmont, Brown, Butler, Carroll, Champaign, Clermont, Clinton, Columbiana, Cuyahoga, Darke, Delaware, Erie, Fayette, Franklin, Geauga, Greene, Hamilton, Harrison, Henry, Licking, Lucas, Madison, Montgomery, Muskingum, Ottawa, Preble, Portage, Picka- way, Ross, Stark, Summit, Trumbull, Tuscarawas, Wash- ington, Warren, and Wayne, in which any such free road is located, a road district for the care and maintenance thereof. (4889, as am., 91 O. L. 355.)

5. *Auditor to give notice to township clerk.* Unless such no- tice has heretofore been given, the auditor of each of said counties must immediately give notice to the clerk of each township in which any such road is located, that the trustees are required to take the charge and control thereof; and the auditor must give the like notice upon the acceptance or appropriation of any other macadamized or graveled road by the county commissioners. (4890.)

6. *Powers of township trustees.* The township clerk, on re- ceipt of such notice from the auditor, must immediately notify the township trustees of such fact, who will, upon receipt of the notice, have full charge and control of all such roads as are herein provided for within their town- ship; and the trustees must divide such road or roads into sections of not less than one-half mile each, and keep them in good repair, and in good condition for all kinds of public travel; and for that purpose they are invested with all necessary powers as to drainage, and the procur- ing and removal of material required for repairs on such roads, as are or may be conferred by law upon supervisors. (4891.)

7. *Trustees may assign roads to supervisors.* The trustees may at their regular March session, each year, apportion and assign to the several supervisors of roads in their townships, such road or roads, or any part or parts thereof, in the road district of such supervisors respectively, to be by them kept in repair, as required in paragraph 6, and under the control and supervision of the trustees. (4892, as am. 81 v. 187.)

8 *Labor and taxes to be set off.* The trustees must pro- vide means for keeping in repair all such roads within their township, and for that purpose must set off persons and districts; such persons must perform their two days' labor as required by law, and also labor in commutation of taxes, the same to be worked out under the direction of such supervisors, or other suitable persons, as provided in paragraphs 6 and 7, and under the control and supervi- sion of the trustees; and such supervisors or persons are authorized to give receipts therefor. The trustees must set off, from the common road fund of their township such amount as seem equitable to them, to be an improved

road fund, especially applicable to the care and improvement of such roads, and may also allow the use of any
plows, scrapers, or other implements owned by the township for road purposes, and do certain other things specified. (4894, as am. 84 v. 85, see par. 3.)

IN ALL OTHER COUNTIES.[1]

9. In every other county, the county commissioners are
constituted a board of directors, in which the management
and control of all such roads, in their respective counties,
is exclusively vested. (4896.)

10. *Board of turnpike directors.* The directors at their
first meeting, must divide the county into three districts,
as nearly equal in number of miles of turnpike, and con-
veniently located, as may be practicable, and each direc-
tor must have the personal supervision of one of such districts, subject to all rules and regulations that may, from
time to time, be agreed upon by the board; and the directors must hold a meeting, as such board, at least once in
three months, at their office at the county seat, and be
governed, in all transactions, by the rules governing
county commissioners. (4897.)

11. The proceedings of these directors must be recorded
in a book, which must be open to the examination of all
persons interested; and they must cause notice to be published, in at least one newspaper of general circulation
throughout the county, of such rules as may be adopted
for the regulation of labor and travel on such roads.[2]
(4898, as am. 81 v. 96.)

12. The directors may appoint suitable persons to super-
intend the work of repairs on these improved roads.
(4898, as am. 81 v. 96.)

13. There is nothing to prevent them from employing the
supervisors of the districts in which such roads lie as such
superintendents, if they are suitable persons. Such superintendents, whether supervisors or not, must be governed by
such lawful rules and instructions as these directors may
adopt and give to the superintendents, and by the laws
governing supervisors, as far as they are applicable.

(1) Champaign and Lucas counties have laws applicable to those
counties only. See 87 v. 198.
(2) They have other rights and duties, which need not be fully
specified here. For instance, they may contract for labor and material, either at public sale or private contract; they may certify to the
county auditor the amount of money needed to keep the roads in repair; they may enter any lands in the county. and take gravel or
other material necessary for the repair of the roads, for which, and
for the damages done by reason of such removal of material,
they must give the owner a certificate, which must be paid for by the
county out of the turnpike fund. Provision is also made for the fixing of the value of this material by the probate court, if the owner is
not satisfied with the amount allowed, and for the levy of taxes for
the benefit of such roads, their collection and expenditure, etc.
(4899-4907.)

14. *Township trustees to apportion road labor.* In townships wherein such roads are located, and placed under the control of turnpike directors under the provisions of this chapter, the township trustees must, at their annual meeting in March, designate and set off such portion of the two days' labor as they may deem just and equitable, to be performed under the control of the board of directors or their superintendents, subject to all the rules and regulations of law for its performance under the direction of road supervisors.[1] (4902.)

15. *Compensation.* The compensation for services of superintendents is subject to the agreement of the board, but not to exceed two dollars and fifty cents per day for time actually employed, and to be paid out of the turnpike fund. (4903.)

16. *Width of tire prescribed.* It is unlawful to transport over the roads mentioned in paragraph 1, page 26, in any vehicle having a tire of less than three inches in width, a burden of more than 2,000 pounds. The county commissioners, acting as turnpike directors, may also prescribe the increased weight in quantity greater than 2,000 pounds, that may be carried in vehicles having a width of tire of three inches or upward, and cause such regulations to be recorded in their journal. It is made the duty of designated officers to prosecute for a violation of the requirements of this section, or of the regulations prescribed by the board, the person or persons violating the same; and said commissioners may appoint some person or persons to enforce, by suit, these provisions, for which such persons are to be paid as further specified in the amended section 4904; in which section injunctions are also provided for; but no duties are prescribed for the supervisor. (4904, as am., 91 O. L. 162.)

17. *Penalties for violation of rules.* Any person who violates, either by himself or agent, any of the rules or regulations adopted by the board, and recorded in their book of records, must, upon conviction thereof before any justice of the peace of the county, or any court having competent jurisdiction, be fined in any sum not less than ten dollars for each offense; and all such fines must be paid into the county treasury for the use of the turnpike fund. (4905.)

18. *Parts of roads in cities and villages to be repaired.* The commissioners must keep in repair such portions of such roads within their respective counties as have since their completion been included, or may hereafter be included, within the corporate limits of any city or village in such counties, to points therein where the sidewalks have been curbed and guttered, and no further. (4906.)

(1) See last part of paragraph 3, this chapter.

II. The Building of Free Turnpikes.

19. *Certain taxes and labor to be applied toward building free turnpikes.* Chapter 7 of the law relating to roads is devoted to "One Mile Assessment Pikes," which are free turnpikes, built at the request of a majority of the holders of land situate within one mile of such roads, from taxes levied on all property so situated. It is only necessary to state here that the law defines what proceedings must be had; that the county commissioners must appoint three freeholders of the county, who are then called road commissioners, and who become a corporation to lay out and establish such a road. All this in no way concerns the supervisor, except so far as stated in the following paragraphs. Though the provisions of these paragraphs are found in the chapter mentioned, yet they are made applicable by section 4812 (as am., 91 O. L. 11), to all free turnpikes, as well as to one mile assessment pikes.

20. So much of any part of the taxes annually levied for road purposes by the trustees of townships, which may be collected within the bounds of any free turnpike road, including the two days' labor authorized by law, must be applied in the construction and repair of the road, under the direction of the road commissioners, or their agents, until the road is completed. (4788.)

21. If, before the completion of the road, the trustees fail to direct the supervisors of any road district, the whole or any part of which is within the bounds of any free turnpike road, to apportion the labor provided for in the preceding paragraph, annually, before the first day of May, and to give notice thereof in writing to the commissioners aforesaid, then all persons liable to do two days' labor, annually, on the public highways, residing within the bounds of any free turnpike road, must do the same under the direction of the commissioners or agents of such road. (4789.)

22. All such persons must perform such labor, after being notified three days previous to the time of doing the same, between the first day of April and the first day of July; but they may pay to the superintendent the sum of three dollars, in lieu of said two days' work, if paid when notified to do the work; and in case of refusal or neglect to do the same, the person so offending shall pay a fine of one dollar, and shall further be liable, in case of non-attendance, to the amount allowed for two days' work, to be collected by the road commissioners, in the same manner that supervisors are authorized to collect in similar cases. (4790.)

23. *When such roads turned over to county commissioners, how kept in repair, etc.* These road commissioners must pros-

ecute for all obstructions or other injuries to such roads while in their charge, and as fast as completed, such road must be turned over to the county commissioners, and must then be kept in repair as stated in the first part of this chapter. (4795, 4796, 4827.)

24. *Road may be made toll road, how and why.* When two consecutive miles or more of any free turnpike road is made in good order for travel or transportation, and the taxes applicable thereto and the two days' labor will not keep the same in repair, the county commissioners may, in the manner prescribed by law, but not necessary to be described here, place toll-gates on such road, and so much toll may be collected as, when added to the common tax of the grand levy and the two days' work, will keep the road in good repair. (4801.)

25. *Who to build bridges, culverts, etc.* When the county commissioners believe the public requires it, they must build any or all bridges and culverts on such roads, and pay for all material used in the construction or repair of such roads, in such manner as they deem best. (4800, as am. 83 v. 167.)

CHAPTER IV.

MISCELLANEOUS PROVISIONS

POINTING OUT WHAT ARE THE DUTIES OF THE SUPERVISOR, AND WHAT ARE NOT IN CERTAIN MATTERS—SOME CRIMINAL LAWS.

1. *Guide-boards.* The township trustees must cause to be erected and kept in repair, at the expense of the township, a post and guide-board, at all such forks and cross-roads as are kept in repair for general public travel, and lead to some village, depot, or other important public place. This guide-board must direct the way and distance to the village, etc., on each of such roads. (4734.)

2. *Watering places—taxes abated.* The township trustees may expend fifty dollars per year in providing and maintaining suitable places for procuring water for persons and animals on the public highways in their township. (4736, as am., 87 O. L. 14.) They must annually abate three dollars from the highway tax of any inhabitant of a road district, who constructs on his own land, and keeps in repair, a watering trough beside the public highway, well supplied with fresh water, the surface of which is two or more feet above the level of the ground, and easily accessible for horses with vehicles. But said trustees may designate the number necessary in each road district, and this tax will be abated for these only. (87 v. 38.)

3. *"Black knot," "peach yellow," etc.* For about a year, the law required road supervisors (and others) when notified in writing by any person that any plum or cherry trees in his district had "black-knot," or that any peach trees had either "peach yellows," or "peach rosettes," to cause such trees to be cut down and burned; or, where practicable, the deceased branches of such trees to be so destroyed each year, as to prevent the spread of said diseases. But this law is now repealed, and provision is made for the appointment of a commission by the township trustees. These commissioners, and the owners of any such trees, have powers, rights, etc., fully provided for by law, which need not be stated fully here. (See 91 v. 108–113.)

4. *How road funds used, etc.* When the township receives money from the county treasury for road purposes, the trustees must cause it to be appropriated to building bridges or repairing roads within their township; and after public notice, let by contract to the lowest bidder (if, in their opinion, he is competent to perform it) such part or parts of any road as they deem expedient, so far as such money will go; and when such labor is performed agreeably to the contract, the trustees must draw an order in favor of the contractor who did said work, to pay for it. (1459)

5. *Bridges and approaches on state and county roads, etc.* The county commissioners must construct and keep in repair all necessary bridges, and the approaches to them, over streams and public canals, on all state and county roads, free turnpikes, improved roads, and abandoned turnpikes and plankroads, except in certain cities and villages.[1] The trustees of the several townships must cause to be built and kept in repair all bridges and culverts, except upon improved and free turnpike roads, when the cost of construction does not exceed fifty dollars, and must keep in repair all bridges constructed by the commissioners; but such repair by said trustees of any such bridge, in any year, must not exceed ten dollars. (860, as am., 91 v. 19; 861, 4940.)

6. *As to overflowed roads.* When any of the principal public roads in any county, except turn-pike toll-roads, are subject to overflow, so as to render them at any time unfit for public travel or transportation, the county commissioners may repair or reconstruct such roads by changing the beds of small streams to avoid crossing, or by changing roads to avoid bridges, or by building embankments sufficiently elevated above all such overflows. (4922, as am., 77 v. 86.)

7. *County commissioners to repair certain damaged highways, how.* When any one or more of the principal highways of any county, or any part of such higways, have been destroyed or damaged by freshet, land-slide, wear, or watercourses or any other casualty, or by the large amount of traffic thereon, or from neglect or inattention to the repair thereof, have become unfit for travel, or cause difficulty, danger, or delay to teams passing thereon, and the commissioners of such county are satisfied that the ordinary levies authorized by law for such purposes will not provide enough money to repair such damages or to remove obstructions from or to make the changes or repairs in such road or roads as are rendered necessary from the causes herein enumerated, said commissioners may annually thereafter, levy a tax at their June session, of any sum not exceeding five mills upon the dollar upon all taxable property of the county, to be expended under their direction in such manner as may seem to them most advantageous to the interest of the county, for the construction, reconstrnction, or repair of such road or roads, or any part thereof. There are other provisions as to levies in this law, which need not be stated here. (See 4919, as am., 91 v. 399.)

8. *Repair of, in certain cases.* When a county road is injured or destroyed by the washing of any lake, river, or creek, or by any washing or sliding of land occasioned by natural drainage, the trustees of the township in which such injury or loss of road has occurred, upon petition of any six freeholders of the township, must call to their aid

[1] Supervisors have nothing to do in or with these cities and villages. See page 6.

a competent surveyor, and proceed to examine such road; and if, upon such examination, the trustees, or a majority of them, are satisfied that such road has been destroyed, or so much injured that the public good requires an altera· tion of the same, they must proceed to alter and lay out so much of the new road as may supply the several parts of the road thus destroyed or injured. (4665.)

9. When the supervisor finds that a county road has been so injured or destroyed, he should not attempt to repair it with the work at his command, but should report it to the trustees for their action.

10. *Sidewalks along roads authorized.* Any person, board of education, village council, cemetery association trustees, or any agricultural or religious society, may appropriate on any public road of sufficient width on either side thereof, sufficient land to construct thereon a public sidewalk not exceeding six feet in width, and may construct such side· walk thereon; but such sidewalks must not obstruct any private entrance or public highway. (4909, as am. 86 v. 33.)

11. *Certain toll-roads may be declared abandoned.* Turnpikes and plankroads, or parts of them, remaining unfinished for five years, or allowed to remain out of repair for six months, may be declared abandoned, and may be appropriated by the county commissioners in such way as the law prescribes. (4913–4918.) But the supervisor will have nothing to do with such abandoned road, until officially notified in writing by the proper authorities. See note 4, page 5.

12. Whenever a public road is crossed by a railroad, the railroad company must erect, at a sufficient elevation from such public road to admit of the free passage of vehicles of every kind, a sign with large and distinct letters placed thereon, to give notice of the nearness of the railroad, and to warn persons to be on the lookout for the locomotive. Such railroad company must also make, at every point where any public road, street, lane, or highway used by the public crosses such railroad, safe and sufficient crossings, and keep the same in good repair; and for any neglect so to do, such company will be liable to all damages to person or property, in any manner caused thereby. (3323, 3324, as amended, 91 O. L. 297.)

13. *Toll-roads may be made free turnpikes—Repairs of.* The law provides that toll-roads owned by private corporations may be purchased and converted into free turnpikes, to be kept in repair as provided in Chapter III; but if the county commissioners are of opinion that such road is not in repair and condition equal to free turnpikes in the vicinity thereof, they are authorized, at their discretion, to assess on the lands taxed for the purchase thereof an amount which will, in their judgment, put it in repair equal to the free turnpikes. (4865–4872.)

14. *Debts not to be contracted by supervisors, etc., without authority.* No officer or agent of the township can make any

contract binding, or purporting to bind the township, to
pay any sum of money not previously appropriated for the
purpose for which such contract is made, and remaining
unexpended and applicable to such purpose, unless he'has
been authorized to make such contract; and if he make
or participate in making a contract without such appropriation or authority, he will be personally liable thereon,
and the township in whose name or behalf the same was
made will not be liable thereon. (17.)

15. *Duties, etc., of supervisors as to hogs running at large.*
It is the duty of all road supervisors, upon view or infor-
mation, to cause all swine found running at large upon
roads within their respective districts to be impounded,
and such further proceedings had as are required by law
in such cases; if any such road supervisor fails or refuses
to perform such duty, he is liable to be fined not less than
two, nor more than five dollars for each offense, to be collected in a suit brought in the name of the State of Ohio,
on complaint of any person feeling aggrieved, before a justice of the peace or other court having jurisdiction where
the offense is committed; and the trustees of the township
are authorized and required to retain, from any sum that
may be due and unpaid to such supervisor for services rendered in his official capacity, any unpaid costs or fines so
arising. He is entitled to fifty cents for each swine so impounded by him. (4203, as amended 77 O. L. 318; 4204,
4208.)

16. *Supervisor's duty as to hedges.* If the owner of any
hedge along a public highway permits such hedge to be
more than six feet high or wide for a longer time than
six months, or leave the cuttings therefrom on the highway longer than ten days, he will be liable to the township trustees in a sum not over fifteen cents per rod of
such hedge; and it is the duty of the supervisor to bring
suit against such owner so offending, before a justice of
the peace of the township in which the hedge is, first giving
such owner twenty days' notice or more, that such hedge
is unlawful, and that unless cut to a proper height within
twenty days, suit will be commenced for such violation.
(4253, 4255.)

SOME CRIMINAL LAWS RELATING TO ROADS AND SUPERSVISORS.

17. Whoever abuses any judge or justice of the peace in
the execution of his office, or knowingly and willfully re-
sists, obstructs, or abuses any sheriff, constable, or other
officer[1], in the execution of his office, shall be fined not
more than five hundred dollars, or imprisoned not more
than thirty days, or both.[2] (6908.)

(1) See note 1, page 1. this book.
(2) Includes supervisor; see note 1, **page 1.**

18. Any supervisor, whether elected or appointed, who embezzles, or converts to his own use, or conceals with such intent, any thing of value that comes into his possession by virtue of his office, or sells any property of the township for his own use, is guilty of embezzlement, and shall be punished as for larceny of the thing embezzled.[1] (6847, 6842, as am. 83 v. 23)

19. Whoever maliciously demolishes, throws down, alters, or defaces any mile-stone, mile-board, mile-post, guide-board, or guide-post, standing on any public road, shall be fined not more than fifty dollars, or imprisoned not more than ten days, or both. (6879.)

20. *Depositing dead animals, offals, etc., into or upon roads, etc.. Duty of supervisor.* Whoever puts the carcass of any dead animal, or the offal from any slaughter-house or butcher's establishment, packing-house, or fish-house, or any spoiled meats, or spoiled fish, or any putrid animal substance, or the contents of any privy vault, upon or into any lake, river, bay, creek, pond, canal, *road*, street, alley, lot, field, meadow, public ground, market space, or common, and whoever, being the owner or occupant of any such place, knowingly permits any such thing to remain therein, to the annoyance of any of the citizens of this state, or neglects or refuses to remove or abate the nuisance occasioned thereby within twenty-four hours after knowledge of the existence of such nuisance upon any of the above described premises owned or occupied by him, or, after notice thereof in writing from any· *supervisor*, constable, trustee, health officer of any municipal corporation or township in which such nuisance exists, or county commissioner, is liable to be fined from ten to fifty dollars, and to thirty days imprisonment. (Part of 6923, as am., 87 O. L. 349.)

21. *Suffering Canada thistles to grow on land or highway.* Whoever knowingly vends any grass or other seed, in or among which there is any seed of the Canada thistle, white or yellow daisey, and whoever, being the owner or possessor of any land, suffers any Canada thistle to grow and ripen seed thereon, or on the highway adjoining the same, shall be fined twenty dollars. (7001.)

22. The owner or operator of any mill, or other manufacturing establishment, near to any public highway, who fails to build or maintain a covert to any water or other wheel attached to such mill or establishment, and exposed to view, shall be fined not more than fifty dollars, and be liable in damages to any person injured in person or property in consequence of the fright or alarm of any animal from the action of such wheel. (7009.)

(1) For the larceny of anything of less value than thirty-five dollars, the penalty is fine of two hundred dollars or less, or imprisonment in the county jail not more than thirty days, or both. If valued at thirty-five dollars or more, imprisonment in penitentiary from one to seven years. (6556.)

23. Whoever, knowing the same to be false or fraudulent, makes out or presents for payment, or certifies as correct, to the general assembly, or to either house thereof, or any committee thereof, or to the auditor of state, or other state officers, or board of officers, or to the auditor or commissioners, or other officers, of any county, or to the auditor or other accounting officer of any municipal corporation, *or to any township trustees, or other township officer,* any claim, bill, note, bond, account, pay-roll, or other evidence of indebtedness, false or fraudulent, in whole or in part, for the purpose of procuring the allowance of the same, or an order for the payment thereof out of the treasury of the said state, county, *township,* or municipal corporation; and whoever, knowing the same to be false, and fraudulent, receives payment of any such claim, account, bill, note, bond, pay-roll, voucher, or other evidence of indebtedness, from the treasurer of the state, or of any county, *township,* or municipal corporation, shall, if such evidence of indebtedness so made out and presented, or certified, or of which payment is received, is false or fraudulent to the amount of thirty-five dollars, or more, be imprisoned in the penitentiary not more than ten years, nor less than one year, or, if false or fraudulent to an amount less than that sum, be fined not more than two hundred dollars, or imprisoned not more than thirty days, or both. (7075.)

24. No supervisor shall directly or indirectly be concerned in any contract for working out the road tax, other than his own, under penalty provided in paragraph 84, page 29. (87 v. 222.) See also said paragraph 84.

INDEX.

(39)

44   INDEX.

FOR THE USE OF ROAD SUPERVISORS.

Abstract of Road Tax.

The township clerk must make out and deliver to each Supervisor an *abstract of the amount of road tax* each person in his district is charged with, as soon as he receives from the county auditor a list of the road tax for his township. (See page 14, this book.)

We sell an abstract specially prepared for this purpose. It contains ruled columns and printed headings for the names of the tax-payers, for the proper description and amount of each one's property liable to taxation, the rate of tax on each dollar, the total road tax (to be filled in by the clerk); also, ruled columns and printed headings for the amount paid in labor by each one, the amount paid in money, the amount still due, and a column in which to write "paid," as the law requires, opposite the names of those who pay in full, either in money or labor. The columns, "Amount paid in labor" and "Amount paid in money," enable the supervisor to keep readily the account of his receipts in cash, which he must account for on his settlement. It also contains printed instructions, laws, etc., and is well and neatly bound in strong glazed pasteboard covers.

Size A (large enough for 125 names), price per copy 10c., per doz. $1.00.

Size B (large enough for 325 names), price per copy 12c., per doz. $1.20.

Larger sizes furnished if required, at slight additional cost.

Supervisor's Bond and Oath.

We have had a new form of bond prepared to meet the demands of the law as now in force. The supervisor's official oath is printed on the same page, each sheet containing two bonds and two oaths, with proper indorsements for filing, etc. As the law now requires this oath and bond each to be recorded by the township clerk in the same book, this arrangement will be found the most convenient and desirable.

Price, per sheet, 5 cents; per quire, 75 cents.

Other Blanks for Supervisors.

Supervisor's certificate or receipt for road tax. Per 100 blanks, 35 cents.

Supervisor's certificate for timber, stone, or other material used. Per quire of 96 blanks, 60 cents.

ROBERT CLALKE & CO., *Publishers*,

61, 63, 65 West Fourth Street,

CINCINNATI.